Forming Consciences

for

Faithful Citizenship

A Call to Political
Responsibility from the

Catholic Bishops
of the United States

with Introductory Note

★ ★ ★

United States Conference of Catholic Bishops
Washington, DC

The document *Forming Consciences for Faithful Citizenship: A Call to Political Responsibility from the Catholic Bishops of the United States* and its Introductory Note were developed by the chairmen, in consultation with the membership, of the Committees on Catholic Education, Communications, Cultural Diversity in the Church, Doctrine, Domestic Justice and Human Development, Evangelization and Catechesis, International Justice and Peace, Migration, Pro-Life Activities; the Subcommittee for the Promotion and Defense of Marriage; and the Ad Hoc Committee for Religious Liberty of the United States Conference of Catholic Bishops (USCCB). It was approved by the full body of bishops at its November 2015 General Meeting. It has been authorized for publication by the undersigned.

Msgr. J. Brian Bransfield
General Secretary, USCCB

ISBN 978-1-60137-528-5

First printing, December 2015

contents

Part III: Goals for Political Life: Challenges for Citizens, Candidates, and Public Officials

Introductory Note

The Catholic bishops of the United States are pleased to offer once again to the Catholic faithful *Forming Consciences for Faithful Citizenship*, our teaching document on the political responsibility of Catholics. This statement represents our guidance for Catholics in the exercise of their rights and duties as participants in our democracy. We urge our pastors, lay and religious faithful, and all people of good will to use this statement to help form their consciences; to teach those entrusted to their care; to contribute to civil and respectful public dialogue; and to shape political choices in the coming election in light of Catholic teaching.

The statement lifts up our dual heritage as both faithful Catholics and American citizens with rights and duties as participants in the civil order. First and foremost, however, we remember that we relate to the civil order as citizens of the heavenly Kingdom, whose reign is not yet fully realized on earth but demands our unqualified allegiance. It is as citizens faithful to the Lord Jesus that we contribute most effectively to the civil order.

This document consists mainly of the statement adopted overwhelmingly by the bishops in 2007, plus certain limited revisions by way of update.

In particular, this version draws on the wealth of papal teaching since the 2007 version of *Faithful Citizenship*, such as the later magisterium of Pope Benedict XVI and that of Pope Francis to date. From these great teachings we discern, for example, messages to the universal Church to attend in a special way: to the inextricable link between our witness to the truth and our service to those in need (*Caritas in Veritate*); to our role as missionary disciples, called forth from the sanctuary to bring Christ to the margins with joy (*Evangelii Gaudium*); and to the care for our common home and all who dwell in it, especially the poorest (*Laudato Si'*).

The document is also updated to take account of recent developments in the United States in both domestic and foreign policy:

- The ongoing destruction of over one million innocent human lives each year by abortion

- Physician-assisted suicide

- The redefinition of marriage—the vital cell of society—by the courts, political bodies, and increasingly by American culture itself

- The excessive consumption of material goods and the destruction of natural resources, which harm both the environment and the poor

- The deadly attacks on fellow Christians and religious minorities throughout the world

- The narrowing redefinition of religious freedom, which threatens both individual conscience and the freedom of the Church to serve

- Economic policies that fail to prioritize the poor, at home or abroad

- A broken immigration system and a worldwide refugee crisis

- Wars, terror, and violence that threaten every aspect of human life and dignity

All of these threats, and more, speak to a breakdown in what Pope Francis has called an "integral ecology" (*Laudato Si'*, nos. 137-55). Without the proper ordering of relationships of persons with each other, with creation, and ultimately with God himself, sin takes hold. Pope Francis reminds us that all individuals, nations, and members of the global community have the duty to place the needs of others ahead of selfish desires to possess and exploit the good things that come from God's hand.

This document is to be read prayerfully and in its totality. It would be a serious mistake—and one that occurs with regrettable frequency—to use only selected parts of the Church's teaching to advance partisan political interests or validate ideological biases. All of us are called to be servants to the whole truth in authentic love, and it is our fervent hope and prayer that this document will provide aid to all those seeking to heed this call.

Finally, while this document is about the civil order, we cannot fail to call the faithful to prayer. The struggles that we face as a nation and as a global community cannot be addressed solely by choosing the "best candidate" for political office. No, in addition to forming our consciences, we must fast and pray, asking our loving and gracious God to give us the ability to effectively proclaim the Gospel of Jesus Christ through our daily witness to our faith and its teachings. Let us all take to heart the urgency of our vocation to live in the service to others through the grace of Christ and ask humbly in prayer for an outpouring of the grace of the Holy Spirit on the United States of America.

PART I

Forming Consciences for Faithful Citizenship: The US Bishops' Reflection on Catholic Teaching and Political Life

Introduction

Our redemption has a social dimension because "God, in Christ, redeems not only the individual person, but also . . . social relations." To believe that the Holy Spirit is at work in everyone means realizing that he seeks to penetrate every human situation and all social bonds. . . . Accepting the first proclamation, which invites us to receive God's love and to love him in return with the very love which is his gift, brings forth in our lives and actions a primary and fundamental response: to desire, seek and protect the good of others.

(Pope Francis, *Evangelii Gaudium*, no. 178)

1. As a nation, we share many blessings and strengths, including a tradition of religious freedom and political participation. However, as a people, we face serious challenges that are both political and moral. This has always been so,

and as Catholics we are called to participate in public life in a manner consistent with the mission of our Lord, a mission that he has called us to share. As Pope Francis teaches,

> An authentic faith . . . always involves a deep desire to change the world, to transmit values, to leave this earth somehow better than we found it. We love this magnificent planet on which God has put us, and we love the human family which dwells here, with all its tragedies and struggles, it hopes and aspirations, its strengths and weaknesses. The earth is our common home and all of us are brothers and sisters. If indeed "the just ordering of society and of the state is a central responsibility of politics," the Church, "cannot and must not remain on the sidelines in the fight for justice." (*Evangelii Gaudium*, no. 183)

In this fight for justice, God gives us a special gift, hope, which Pope Benedict describes in *Caritas in Veritate* as "burst[ing] into our lives as something not due to us, something that transcends every law of justice" (no. 34). Thus we take up the task of serving the common good with joy and hope, confident that God, who "so loved the world that he gave his only Son," walks with us and strengthens us on the way (Jn 3:16). God is love, and he desires that we help to build a "civilization of love"—one in which all human beings have the freedom and opportunity to experience the love of God and live out that love by making a free gift of themselves to one another. Pope Francis encourages us in *Evangelii Gaudium* to meditate on the

> inseparable bond between our acceptance of the message of salvation and genuine fraternal love . . . God's word teaches that our brothers and sisters are the prolongation of the incarnation for each of us: "As you did it to one of these, the least of my brethren, you did it to me" (Mt 25:40). The way we treat others has a transcendent dimension: "The measure you give will be the measure you get" (Mt 7:2). It corresponds to the mercy which God has shown us: "Be merciful, just as your Father is merciful. Do not judge, and you will not be judged; do not condemn, and you will not be condemned. Forgive, and you will be forgiven; give, and it will be given to

you . . . For the measure you give will be the measure you get back" (Lk 6:36-38). What these passages make clear is the absolute priority of "going forth from ourselves toward our brothers and sisters" as one of the two great commandments which ground every moral norm and as the clearest sign for discerning spiritual growth in response to God's completely free gift. (no. 179)

Love compels us "to 'go into all the world and proclaim the good news to the whole creation' (Mk 16:15)" (*Evangelii Gaudium*, no. 181). "Here," Pope Francis continues, "'the creation' refers to every aspect of human life; consequently, 'the mission of proclaiming the good news of Jesus Christ has a universal destination. Its mandate of charity encompasses all dimensions of existence, all individuals, all areas of community life, and all peoples. Nothing human can be alien to it'" (*Evangelii Gaudium*, no. 181). This "mandate" includes our engagement in political life.

2. The political realities of our nation present us with opportunities and challenges. We are a nation founded on "life, liberty, and the pursuit of happiness," but the right to life itself is not fully protected, especially for unborn children, the terminally ill, and the elderly, the most vulnerable members of the American family. We are called to be peacemakers in a nation at war. We are a country pledged to pursue "liberty and justice for all," but we are too often divided across lines of race, ethnicity, and economic inequality. We are a nation of immigrants, struggling to address the challenges of many new immigrants in our midst. We are a society built on the strength of our families, called to defend marriage and offer moral and economic supports for family life. We are a powerful nation in a violent world, confronting terror and trying to build a safer, more just, more peaceful world. We are an affluent society where too many live in poverty and lack health care and other necessities of life. We are part of a global community charged with being good stewards of the earth's environment, what Pope Francis calls "our common home," which is being threatened. These challenges are at the heart of public life and at the center of the pursuit of the common good.[1] They are intertwined and inseparable. As Pope Francis has insisted, "We are faced . . . with one complex crisis which is both social and environmental. Strategies for a solution demand an integrated approach to combating poverty, restoring dignity to the excluded, and at the same time protecting nature" (*Laudato Si'*, no. 139).

3

faithful citizenship

3. For many years, we bishops of the United States have sought to share Catholic teaching on social and political life. We have done so in a series of statements issued every four years focused on "political responsibility" or "faithful citizenship." In this document we continue that practice, maintaining continuity with what we have said in the past in light of new challenges facing our nation and world. This is not new teaching but affirms what is taught by our bishops' conference and the whole Church.

4. As Catholics, we are part of a community with a rich heritage that helps us consider the challenges in public life and contribute to greater justice and peace for all people. Part of that rich heritage on faithful citizenship is the teaching of Vatican Council II's *Declaration on Religious Liberty* (*Dignitatis Humanae*). It says that "society itself may profit by the moral qualities of justice and peace which have their origin in [people's] faithfulness to God and to His holy will" (no. 6). The work for justice requires that the mind and the heart of Catholics be educated and formed to know and practice the whole faith.

5. This statement highlights the role of the Church in the formation of conscience and the corresponding moral responsibility of each Catholic to hear, receive, and act upon the Church's teaching in the lifelong task of forming his or her own conscience. Foremost amongst those teachings are the four basic principles of Catholic social doctrine: the dignity of the human person, the common good, subsidiarity, and solidarity (*Compendium of the Social Doctrine of the Church*, no. 160). With this foundation, Catholics are better able to evaluate policy positions, party platforms, and candidates' promises and actions in light of the Gospel and the moral and social teaching of the Church in order to help build a better world.

6. We seek to do this by addressing four questions: (1) Why does the Church teach about issues affecting public policy? (2) Who in the Church should participate in political life? (3) How does the Church help the Catholic faithful to speak about political and social questions? (4) What does the Church say about Catholic social teaching in the public square?

7. In this statement, we bishops do not intend to tell Catholics for whom or against whom to vote. Our purpose is to help Catholics form their consciences in accordance with God's truth. We recognize that the responsibility to make choices in political life rests with each individual in light of a properly formed conscience, and that participation goes well beyond casting a vote in a particular election.

8. During election years, there may be many handouts and voter guides that are produced and distributed. We encourage Catholics to seek those resources authorized by their own bishops, their state Catholic conferences, and the United States Conference of Catholic Bishops. This statement is intended to reflect and complement, not substitute for, the ongoing teaching of bishops in our own dioceses and states. When using this document, it is important to remember that Church teaching is coherent and rests on a comprehensive vision of the dignity of the human person, a dignity that St. John Paul II described as "manifested in all its radiance when the person's origin and destiny are considered: created by God in his image and likeness as well as redeemed by the most precious blood of Christ, the person is called to be a 'child in the Son' and a living temple of the Spirit, destined for the eternal life of blessed communion with God" (*Christifideles Laici*, no. 37). Thus, the particular judgments of the document may fall at various points along the political spectrum, but the foundational principles that guide these teachings should not be ignored in any case nor used selectively in order to serve partisan interests. In light of these reflections and those of local bishops, we encourage Catholics throughout the United States to be active in the political process, particularly in these challenging times.

Why Does the Church Teach About Issues Affecting Public Policy?

The Church's teachings concerning contingent situations are subject to new and further developments and can be open to discussion, yet we cannot help but be concrete—without presuming to enter into details—lest the great social principles remain mere generalities which challenge no one. . . . The Church's pastors, taking into account the contributions of the different sciences, have the right to offer opinions in all that affects people's lives, since the task of evangelization implies and demands the integral promotion of each human being.

(Pope Francis, *Evangelii Gaudium*, no. 182)

9. The Church's obligation to participate in shaping the moral character of society is a requirement of our faith. It is a basic part of the mission we have received from Jesus Christ, who offers a vision of life revealed to us in Sacred Scripture and Tradition. To echo the teaching of the Second Vatican Council: Christ, the Word made flesh, in showing us the Father's love, also shows us what it truly means to be human (see *Gaudium et Spes*, no. 22). Christ's love for us lets us see our human dignity in full clarity and compels us to love our neighbors as he has loved us. Christ, the Teacher, shows us what is true and

good, that is, what is in accord with our human nature as free, intelligent beings created in God's image and likeness and endowed by the Creator with dignity and rights as well as duties.

Christ also reveals to us the weaknesses that are part of all human endeavors. In the language of revelation, we are confronted with sin, both personal and structural. "The Church's wisdom," according to Pope Benedict XVI, "has always pointed to the presence of original sin in social conditions and in the structure of society" (*Caritas in Veritate*, no. 34). All "structures of sin," as St. John Paul II calls them, "are rooted in personal sin, and thus always linked to the concrete acts of individuals who introduce these structures, consolidate them and make them difficult to remove" (*Sollicitudo Rei Socialis*, no. 36). Thus, our faith helps us understand that the pursuit of a civilization of love must address our own failures and the ways in which these failures distort the broader ordering of the society in which we live. In the words of the *Catechism of the Catholic Church*, "Ignorance of the fact that man has a wounded nature inclined to evil gives rise to serious errors in the areas of education, politics, social action and morals" (no. 407). As Pope Francis, quoting Pope Benedict XVI, reaffirmed in *Evangelii Gaudium*, "We need to be convinced that charity 'is the principle not only of micro-relationships (with friends, with family members or within small groups) but also of macro-relationships (social, economic and political ones)'" (no. 205).

10. What faith teaches about the dignity of the human person, about the sacredness of every human life, and about humanity's strengths and weaknesses helps us see more clearly the same truths that also come to us through the gift of human reason. At the center of these truths is respect for the dignity of every person. This is the core of Catholic moral and social teaching. Because we are people of both faith and reason, it is appropriate and necessary for us to bring this essential truth about human life and dignity to the public square. We are called to practice Christ's commandment to "love one another" (Jn 13:34). We are also called to promote the well-being of all, to share our blessings with those most in need, to defend marriage, and to protect the lives and dignity of all, especially the weak, the vulnerable, the voiceless. In his first encyclical letter, *Deus Caritas Est*, Pope Benedict XVI explained that "charity must animate the entire lives of the lay faithful and therefore also their political activity, lived as 'social charity'" (no. 29).

11. Some question whether it is appropriate for the Church to play a role in political life. However, the obligation to teach the moral truths that should shape our lives, including our public lives, is central to the mission given to the Church by Jesus Christ. Moreover, the United States Constitution protects

the right of individual believers and religious bodies to participate and speak out without government interference, favoritism, or discrimination. Civil law should fully recognize and protect the right of the Church and other institutions in civil society to participate in cultural, political, and economic life without being forced to abandon or ignore their central moral convictions. Our nation's tradition of pluralism is enhanced, not threatened, when religious groups and people of faith bring their convictions and concerns into public life. Indeed, our Church's teaching is in accord with the foundational values that have shaped our nation's history: "life, liberty, and the pursuit of happiness."

12. The Catholic community brings important assets to the political dialogue about our nation's future. We bring a consistent moral framework—drawn from basic human reason that is illuminated by Scripture and the teaching of the Church—for assessing issues, political platforms, and campaigns. We also bring broad experience in serving those in need—educating the young, serving families in crisis, caring for the sick, sheltering the homeless, helping women who face difficult pregnancies, feeding the hungry, welcoming immigrants and refugees, reaching out in global solidarity, and pursuing peace. We celebrate, with all our neighbors, the historically robust commitment to religious freedom in this country that has allowed the Church the freedom to serve the common good.

Who in the Church Should Participate in Political Life?

Laymen should also know that it is generally the function of their well-formed Christian conscience to see that the divine law is inscribed in the life of the earthly city; from priests they may look for spiritual light and nourishment. . . . Since they have an active role to play in the whole life of the Church, laymen are not only bound to penetrate the world with a Christian spirit, but are also called to be witnesses to Christ in all things in the midst of human society.

Bishops, to whom is assigned the task of ruling the Church of God, should, together with their priests, so preach the news of Christ that all the earthly activities of the faithful will be bathed in the light of the Gospel. All pastors should remember too that by their daily conduct and concern they are revealing the face of the Church to the world, and men will judge the power and truth of the Christian message thereby.

(Second Vatican Council, *Gaudium et Spes*, no. 43)

13. In the Catholic Tradition, responsible citizenship is a virtue, and participation in political life is a moral obligation. "People in every nation enhance the

social dimension of their lives by acting as committed and responsible citizens" (*Evangelii Gaudium*, no. 220). The obligation to participate in political life is rooted in our baptismal commitment to follow Jesus Christ and to bear Christian witness in all we do. As the *Catechism of the Catholic Church* reminds us, "It is necessary that all participate, each according to his position and role, in promoting the common good. This obligation is inherent in the dignity of the human person. . . . As far as possible citizens should take an active part in public life" (nos. 1913-1915).

14. Unfortunately, politics in our country often can be a contest of powerful interests, partisan attacks, sound bites, and media hype. The Church calls for a different kind of political engagement: one shaped by the moral convictions of well-formed consciences and focused on the dignity of every human being, the pursuit of the common good, and the protection of the weak and the vulnerable. As Pope Francis reminds us, "Politics, though often denigrated, remains a lofty vocation and one of the highest forms of charity, inasmuch as it seeks the common good. . . . I beg the Lord to grant us more politicians who are genuinely disturbed by the state of society, the people, the lives of the poor!" (*Evangelii Gaudium*, no. 205). The Catholic call to faithful citizenship affirms the importance of political participation and insists that public service is a worthy vocation. As citizens, we should be guided more by our moral convictions than by our attachment to a political party or interest group. When necessary, our participation should help transform the party to which we belong; we should not let the party transform us in such a way that we neglect or deny fundamental moral truths or approve intrinsically evil acts. We are called to bring together our principles and our political choices, our values and our votes, to help build a civilization of truth and love.

15. Clergy and lay people have complementary roles in public life. We bishops have the primary responsibility to hand on the Church's moral and social teaching. Together with priests and deacons, assisted by religious and lay leaders of the Church, we are to teach fundamental moral principles that help Catholics form their consciences correctly, to provide guidance on the moral dimensions of public decisions, and to encourage the faithful to carry out their responsibilities in political life. In fulfilling these responsibilities, the Church's leaders avoid endorsing or opposing candidates. As Pope Benedict XVI stated in *Deus Caritas Est*,

> The Church wishes to help form consciences in political life and to stimulate greater insight into the authentic require-

ments of justice as well as greater readiness to act accordingly, even when this might involve conflict with situations of personal interest. . . . The Church cannot and must not take upon herself the political battle to bring about the most just society possible. She cannot and must not replace the State. Yet at the same time she cannot and must not remain on the sidelines in the fight for justice. (no. 28)

16. As the Holy Father also taught in *Deus Caritas Est*, "The direct duty to work for a just ordering of society is proper to the lay faithful" (no. 29). This duty is more critical than ever in today's political environment, where Catholics may feel politically disenfranchised, sensing that no party and too few candidates fully share the Church's comprehensive commitment to the life and dignity of every human being from conception to natural death. Yet this is not a time for retreat or discouragement; rather, it is a time for renewed engagement. Forming their consciences in accord with Catholic teaching, Catholic lay women and men can become actively involved: running for office; working within political parties; communicating their concerns and positions to elected officials; and joining diocesan social mission or advocacy networks, state Catholic conference initiatives, community organizations, and other efforts to apply authentic moral teaching in the public square. Even those who cannot vote have the right to have their voices heard on issues that affect their lives and the common good.

How Does the Church Help the Catholic Faithful to Speak About Political and Social Questions?

As the bishops of the United States of America have rightly pointed out, while the Church insists on the existence of objective moral norms which are valid for everyone, "there are those in our culture who portray this teaching as unjust, that is, as opposed to basic human rights. Such claims usually follow from a form of moral relativism that is joined, not without inconsistency, to a belief in the absolute rights of individuals. In this view, the Church is perceived as promoting a particular prejudice and as interfering with individual freedom" (USCCB, Ministry to Persons with a Homosexual Inclination (2006), 17). We are living in an information-driven society which bombards us indiscriminately with data—all treated as being of equal importance—and which leads to remarkable superficiality in the area of moral dis-

cernment. In response, we need to provide an education which teaches critical think-ing and encourages the development of mature moral values.

(Pope Francis, *Evangelii Gaudium*, no. 64)

A Well-Formed Conscience

17. The Church equips its members to address political and social questions by helping them to develop a well-formed conscience. Catholics have a serious and lifelong obligation to form their consciences in accord with human reason and the teaching of the Church. Conscience is not something that allows us to justify doing whatever we want, nor is it a mere "feeling" about what we should or should not do. Rather, conscience is the voice of God resounding in the human heart, revealing the truth to us and calling us to do what is good while shunning what is evil. Conscience always requires serious attempts to make sound moral judgments based on the truths of our faith. As stated in the *Catechism of the Catholic Church*, "Conscience is a judgment of reason whereby the human person recognizes the moral quality of a concrete act that he is going to perform, is in the process of performing, or has already completed. In all he says and does, man is obliged to follow faithfully what he knows to be just and right" (no. 1778).

18. The formation of conscience includes several elements. First, there is a desire to embrace goodness and truth. For Catholics, this begins with a will-ingness and openness to seek the truth and what is right by studying Sacred Scripture and the teaching of the Church as contained in the *Catechism of the Catholic Church*. It is also important to examine the facts and background information about various choices. Finally, prayerful reflection is essential to discern the will of God. Catholics must also understand that if they fail to form their consciences in the light of the truths of the faith and the moral teachings of the Church they can make erroneous judgments.[2]

The Virtue of Prudence

19. The Church fosters well-formed consciences not only by teaching moral truth but also by encouraging its members to develop the virtue of prudence, which St. Ambrose described as "the charioteer of the virtues." Prudence enables us "to discern our true good in every circumstance and to choose the right means of achieving it" (*Catechism of the Catholic Church*, no. 1806). Pru-dence shapes and informs our ability to deliberate over available alternatives,

to determine what is most fitting to a specific context, and to act decisively. Exercising this virtue often requires the courage to act in defense of moral principles when making decisions about how to build a society of justice and peace.

20. The Church's teaching is clear that a good end does not justify an immoral means. As we all seek to advance the common good—by defending the inviolable sanctity of human life from the moment of conception until natural death, by promoting religious freedom, by defending marriage, by feeding the hungry and housing the homeless, by welcoming the immigrant and protecting the environment—it is important to recognize that not all possible courses of action are morally acceptable. We have a responsibility to discern carefully which public policies are morally sound. Catholics may choose different ways to respond to compelling social problems, but we cannot differ on our moral obligation to help build a more just and peaceful world through morally acceptable means, so that the weak and vulnerable are protected and human rights and dignity are defended.

Doing Good and Avoiding Evil

21. Aided by the virtue of prudence in the exercise of well-formed consciences, Catholics are called to make practical judgments regarding good and evil choices in the political arena.

22. There are some things we must never do, as individuals or as a society, because they are always incompatible with love of God and neighbor. Such actions are so deeply flawed that they are always opposed to the authentic good of persons. These are called "intrinsically evil" actions. They must always be rejected and opposed and must never be supported or condoned. A prime example is the intentional taking of innocent human life, as in abortion and euthanasia. In our nation, "abortion and euthanasia have become preeminent threats to human dignity because they directly attack life itself, the most fundamental human good and the condition for all others" (*Living the Gospel of Life*, no. 5). It is a mistake with grave moral consequences to treat the destruction of innocent human life merely as a matter of individual choice. A legal system that violates the basic right to life on the grounds of choice is fundamentally flawed.

23. Similarly, human cloning, destructive research on human embryos, and other acts that directly violate the sanctity and dignity of human life are also

intrinsically evil. These must always be opposed. Other direct assaults on innocent human life, such as genocide, torture, and the targeting of noncombatants in acts of terror or war, can never be justified. Nor can violations of human dignity, such as acts of racism, treating workers as mere means to an end, deliberately subjecting workers to subhuman living conditions, treating the poor as disposable, or redefining marriage to deny its essential meaning, ever be justified.

24. Opposition to intrinsically evil acts, which undercut the dignity of the human person, should also open our eyes to the good we must do, that is, to our positive duty to contribute to the common good and to act in solidarity with those in need. As St. John Paul II said, "The fact that only the negative commandments oblige always and under all circumstances does not mean that in the moral life prohibitions are more important than the obligation to do good indicated by the positive commandment" (*Veritatis Splendor*, no. 52). Both opposing evil *and* doing good are essential obligations.

25. The right to life implies and is linked to other human rights—to the basic goods that every human person needs to live and thrive. All the life issues are connected, for erosion of respect for the life of any individual or group in society necessarily diminishes respect for all life. The moral imperative to respond to the needs of our neighbors—basic needs such as food, shelter, health care, education, and meaningful work—is universally binding on our consciences and may be legitimately fulfilled by a variety of means. Catholics must seek the best ways to respond to these needs. As St. John XXIII taught, "[Each of us] has the right to life, to bodily integrity, and to the means which are suitable for the proper development of life; these are primarily food, clothing, shelter, rest, medical care, and, finally, the necessary social services" (*Pacem in Terris*, no. 11).

26. St. John Paul II explained the importance of being true to fundamental Church teachings:

> Above all, the common outcry, which is justly made on
> behalf of human rights—for example, the right to health, to
> home, to work, to family, to culture—is false and illusory if
> *the right to life*, the most basic and fundamental right and the

condition for all other personal rights, is not defended with maximum determination. (*Christifideles Laici*, no. 38)

27. Two temptations in public life can distort the Church's defense of human life and dignity:

28. The first is a moral equivalence that makes no ethical distinctions between different kinds of issues involving human life and dignity. The direct and intentional destruction of innocent human life from the moment of conception until natural death is always wrong and is not just one issue among many. It must always be opposed.[3]

29. The second is the misuse of these necessary moral distinctions as a way of dismissing or ignoring other serious threats to human life and dignity. The current and projected extent of environmental degradation has become a moral crisis especially because it poses a risk to humanity in the future and threatens the lives of poor and vulnerable human persons here and now. Racism and other unjust discrimination, the use of the death penalty, resorting to unjust war, the use of torture,[4] war crimes, the failure to respond to those who are suffering from hunger or a lack of health care, pornography, redefining civil marriage, compromising religious liberty, or an unjust immigration policy are all serious moral issues that challenge our consciences and require us to act. These are not optional concerns which can be dismissed. Catholics are urged to seriously consider Church teaching on these issues. Although choices about how best to respond to these and other compelling threats to human life and dignity are matters for principled debate and decision, this does not make them optional concerns or permit Catholics to dismiss or ignore Church teaching on these important issues. Clearly not every Catholic can be actively involved on each of these concerns, but we need to support one another as our community of faith defends human life and dignity wherever it is threatened. We are not factions, but one family of faith fulfilling the mission of Jesus Christ.

30. The Vatican Congregation for the Doctrine of the Faith made a similar point:

> It must be noted also that a well-formed Christian conscience does not permit one to vote for a political program or an individual law which contradicts the fundamental

contents of faith and morals. The Christian faith is an integral unity, and thus it is incoherent to isolate some particular element to the detriment of the whole of Catholic doctrine. A political commitment to a single isolated aspect of the Church's social doctrine does not exhaust one's responsibility toward the common good. (*Doctrinal Note on Some Questions Regarding the Participation of Catholics in Political Life*, no. 4)

Making Moral Choices

31. Decisions about political life are complex and require the exercise of a well-formed conscience aided by prudence. This exercise of conscience begins with outright opposition to laws and other policies that violate human life or weaken its protection. Those who knowingly, willingly, and directly support public policies or legislation that undermine fundamental moral principles cooperate with evil.

32. Sometimes morally flawed laws already exist. In this situation, the process of framing legislation to protect life is subject to prudential judgment and "the art of the possible." At times this process may restore justice only partially or gradually. For example, St. John Paul II taught that when a government official who fully opposes abortion cannot succeed in completely overturning a pro-abortion law, he or she may work to improve protection for unborn human life, "limiting the harm done by such a law" and lessening its negative impact as much as possible (*Evangelium Vitae*, no. 73). Such incremental improvements in the law are acceptable as steps toward the full restoration of justice. However, Catholics must never abandon the moral requirement to seek full protection for all human life from the moment of conception until natural death.

33. Prudential judgment is also needed in applying moral principles to specific policy choices in areas such as armed conflict, housing, health care, immigration, and others. This does not mean that all choices are equally valid, or that our guidance and that of other Church leaders is just another political opinion or policy preference among many others. Rather, we urge Catholics to listen carefully to the Church's teachers when we apply Catholic social teaching to specific proposals and situations. The judgments and recommendations that we make as bishops on such specific issues do not carry the same moral authority as statements of universal moral teachings. Nevertheless, the Church's

guidance on these matters is an essential resource for Catholics as they determine whether their own moral judgments are consistent with the Gospel and with Catholic teaching.

34. Catholics often face difficult choices about how to vote. This is why it is so important to vote according to a well-formed conscience that perceives the proper relationship among moral goods. A Catholic cannot vote for a candidate who favors a policy promoting an intrinsically evil act, such as abortion, euthanasia, assisted suicide, deliberately subjecting workers or the poor to sub-human living conditions, redefining marriage in ways that violate its essential meaning, or racist behavior, if the voter's intent is to support that position. In such cases, a Catholic would be guilty of formal cooperation in grave evil. At the same time, a voter should not use a candidate's opposition to an intrinsic evil to justify indifference or inattentiveness to other important moral issues involving human life and dignity.

35. There may be times when a Catholic who rejects a candidate's unacceptable position even on policies promoting an intrinsically evil act may reasonably decide to vote for that candidate for other morally grave reasons. Voting in this way would be permissible only for truly grave moral reasons, not to advance narrow interests or partisan preferences or to ignore a fundamental moral evil.

36. When all candidates hold a position that promotes an intrinsically evil act, the conscientious voter faces a dilemma. The voter may decide to take the extraordinary step of not voting for any candidate or, after careful deliberation, may decide to vote for the candidate deemed less likely to advance such a morally flawed position and more likely to pursue other authentic human goods.

37. In making these decisions, it is essential for Catholics to be guided by a well-formed conscience that recognizes that all issues do not carry the same moral weight and that the moral obligation to oppose policies promoting intrinsically evil acts has a special claim on our consciences and our actions. These decisions should take into account a candidate's commitments, character, integrity, and ability to influence a given issue. In the end, this is a decision to be made by each Catholic guided by a conscience formed by Catholic moral teaching.

38. It is important to be clear that the political choices faced by citizens not only have an impact on general peace and prosperity but also may affect the individual's salvation. Similarly, the kinds of laws and policies supported by public officials affect their spiritual well-being. Pope Benedict XVI, in his reflection on the Eucharist as "the sacrament of charity," challenged all of us to adopt what he calls "a Eucharistic form of life." This means that the redeeming love we encounter in the Eucharist should shape our thoughts, our words, and our decisions, including those that pertain to the social order. The Holy Father called for "Eucharistic consistency" on the part of every member of the Church:

> It is important to consider what the Synod Fathers described as *eucharistic consistency*, a quality which our lives are objectively called to embody. Worship pleasing to God can never be a purely private matter, without consequences for our relationships with others: it demands a public witness to our faith. Evidently, this is true for all the baptized, yet it is especially incumbent upon those who, by virtue of their social or political position, must make decisions regarding fundamental values, such as respect for human life, its defense from conception to natural death, the family built upon marriage between a man and a woman, the freedom to educate one's children and the promotion of the common good in all its forms. . . . (*Sacramentum Caritatis*, no. 83)

39. This calls for a heroic commitment on the part of Catholics who are politicians and other leaders in society. Having been entrusted with special responsibility for the common good, Catholic leaders must commit themselves to the pursuit of the virtues, especially courage, justice, temperance, and prudence. The culmination of these virtues is the strong public promotion of the dignity of every human person as made in the image of God in accord with the teachings of the Church, even when it conflicts with current public opinion. Catholic politicians and legislators must recognize their grave responsibility in society to support laws shaped by these fundamental human values and oppose laws and policies that violate life and dignity at any stage from conception to natural death. This is not to bring a "Catholic interest" to the political sphere, it is to insist that the truth of the dignity of the human

person, as discovered by reason and confirmed by revelation, be at the forefront of all political considerations.

What Does the Church Say About Catholic Social Teaching in the Public Square?—Four Principles of Catholic Social Teaching

The permanent principles of the Church's social doctrine constitute the very heart of Catholic social teaching. These are the principles of: the dignity of the human person, . . . the common good; subsidiarity; and solidarity. These principles [are] the expression of the whole truth about man known by reason and faith . . ."

(*Compendium of the Social Doctrine of the Church*, no. 160)

40. In the words of Pope Francis, "progress in building a people in peace, justice and fraternity depends on four principles related to constant tensions present in every social reality. These derive from the pillars of the Church's social doctrine, which serve as 'primary and fundamental parameters of reference for interpreting and evaluating social phenomena'" (*Evangelii Gaudium*, no. 221). Taken together, these principles provide a moral framework for Catholic engagement in advancing what we have called elsewhere a "consistent ethic of life" (*Living the Gospel of Life*, no. 22). Rightly understood, this ethic does not treat all issues as morally equivalent nor does it reduce Catholic teaching to one or two issues. It anchors the Catholic commitment to defend human life, from conception until natural death, in the fundamental moral obligation to respect the dignity of every person as a child of God. It unites us as a "people of life and for life" (*Evangelium Vitae*, no. 6) pledged to build what St. John Paul II called a "culture of life" (*Evangelium Vitae*, no. 77). This culture of life begins with the preeminent obligation to protect innocent life from direct attack and extends to defending life whenever it is threatened or diminished:

> Any politics of human dignity must seriously address issues
> of racism, poverty, hunger, employment, education, housing,
> and health care. . . . If we understand the human person as
> the "temple of the Holy Spirit"—the living house of God—
> then these issues fall logically into place as the crossbeams

and walls of that house. *All direct attacks on innocent human life, such as abortion and euthanasia, strike at the house's foundation.* (*Living the Gospel of Life*, no. 22)

41. Catholic voters should use the framework of Catholic social teaching to examine candidates' positions on issues affecting human life and dignity as well as issues of justice and peace, and they should consider candidates' integrity, philosophy, and performance. It is important for all citizens "to see beyond party politics, to analyze campaign rhetoric critically, and to choose their political leaders according to principle, not party affiliation or mere self-interest" (*Living the Gospel of Life*, no. 33).

42. As Catholics we are not single-issue voters. A candidate's position on a single issue is not sufficient to guarantee a voter's support. Yet if a candidate's position on a single issue promotes an intrinsically evil act, such as legal abortion, redefining marriage in a way that denies its essential meaning, or racist behavior, a voter may legitimately disqualify a candidate from receiving support.

43. As noted previously, the Catholic approach to faithful citizenship rests on moral principles found in Sacred Scripture and Catholic moral and social teaching as well as in the hearts of all people of good will. Recent papal teaching has identified four major principles of Catholic social teaching. We now present the central and enduring themes of the Catholic social tradition organized under these four principles that can provide a moral framework for decisions in public life.[5]

The Dignity of the Human Person

44. Human life is sacred. The **dignity of the human person** is the foundation of a moral vision for society. Direct attacks on innocent persons are never morally acceptable, at any stage or in any condition. In our society, human life is especially under direct attack from abortion, which some political actors mischaracterize as an issue of "women's health." Other direct threats to the sanctity of human life include euthanasia and assisted suicide (sometimes falsely labelled as "death with dignity"), human cloning, in vitro fertilization, and the destruction of human embryos for research.

45. Catholic teaching about the dignity of life calls us to oppose torture,[6] unjust war, and the indiscriminate use of drones for violent purposes; to prevent genocide and attacks against noncombatants; to oppose racism; to oppose human trafficking; and to overcome poverty and suffering. Nations are called to protect the right to life by seeking effective ways to combat evil and terror without resorting to armed conflicts except as a last resort after all peaceful means have failed, and to end the use of the death penalty as a means of protecting society from violent crime. We revere the lives of children in the womb, the lives of persons dying in war and from starvation, and indeed the lives of all human beings as children of God. We stand opposed to these and all activities that contribute to what Pope Francis has called "a throwaway culture."

Subsidiarity

It is impossible to promote the dignity of the person without showing concern for the family, groups, associations, local territorial realities; in short, for that aggregate of economic, social, cultural, sports-oriented, recreational, professional and political expressions to which people spontaneously give life and which make it possible for them to achieve effective social growth.

(*Compendium of the Social Doctrine of the Church*, no. 185)

46. The human person is not only sacred but also social. Full human development takes place in relationship with others. The **family**—based on marriage between a man and a woman—is the first and fundamental unit of society and is a sanctuary for the creation and nurturing of children. It should be defended and strengthened, not redefined, undermined, or further distorted. Respect for the family should be reflected in every policy and program. It is important to uphold parents' rights and responsibilities to care for their children, including the right to choose their children's education.

47. How we organize our society—in economics and politics, in law and policy—directly affects the common good and the capacity of individuals to develop their full potential. Every person and association has a right and a duty to participate actively in shaping society and to promote the well-being of all, especially the poor and vulnerable.

48. The principle of subsidiarity reminds us that larger institutions in society should not overwhelm or interfere with smaller or local institutions, yet larger institutions have essential responsibilities when the more local institutions cannot adequately protect human dignity, meet human needs, and advance the common good (*Centesimus Annus*, no. 48; *Dignitatis Humanae*, nos. 4-6).

The Common Good

The common good indicates "the sum total of social conditions which allow people, either as groups or as individuals, to reach their fulfilment more fully and more easily" (Gaudium et Spes, no. 26). . . . The common good, in fact, can be understood as the social and community dimension of the moral good.

(*Compendium of the Social Doctrine of the Church*, no. 164)

49. Human dignity is respected and the common good is fostered only if **human rights are protected and basic responsibilities** are met. Every human being has a right to life, the fundamental right that makes all other rights possible, and a right to access those things required for human decency—food and shelter, education and employment, health care and housing, freedom of religion and family life. The right to exercise religious freedom publicly and privately by individuals and institutions along with freedom of conscience need to be constantly defended. In a fundamental way, the right to free expression of religious beliefs protects all other rights. Corresponding to these rights are duties and responsibilities—to one another, to our families, and to the larger society. Rights should be understood and exercised in a moral framework rooted in the dignity of the human person.

50. The economy must serve people, not the other way around. It is therefore necessary that an economic system serve the dignity of the human person and the common good by respecting the **dignity of work and protecting the rights of workers**. A "growth in justice," according to Pope Francis in *Evangelii Gaudium*,

> requires more than economic growth, while presupposing such growth: it requires decisions, programs, mechanisms and processes specifically geared to a better distribution

of income, the creation of sources of employment and an integral promotion of the poor which goes beyond a simple welfare mentality. I am far from proposing an irresponsible populism, but the economy can no longer turn to remedies that are a new poison, such as attempting to increase profits by reducing the work force and thereby adding to the ranks of the excluded. (no. 204)

Work is more than a way to make a living; it is a form of continuing participation in God's creation. Employers contribute to the common good through the services or products they provide and by creating jobs that uphold the dignity and rights of workers—to productive work, to decent and just wages, to adequate benefits and security in their old age, to the choice of whether to organize and join unions, to the opportunity for legal status for immigrant workers, to private property, and to economic initiative. Workers also have responsibilities—to provide a fair day's work for a fair day's pay, to treat employers and co-workers with respect, and to carry out their work in ways that contribute to the common good. Workers, employers, and unions should not only advance their own interests but also work together to advance economic justice and the well-being of all. Pope Francis has summarized well the Church's teaching on work in *Laudato Si'*. "Work," he writes,

> should be the setting for . . . rich personal growth, where many aspects of life enter into play: creativity, planning for the future, developing our talents, living out our values, relating to others, giving glory to God. . . . Work is a necessity, part of the meaning of life on this earth, a path to growth, human development and personal fulfillment. Helping the poor financially must always be a provisional solution in the face of pressing needs. The broader objective should always be to allow them a dignified life through work. (*Laudato Si'*, no. 127-128)

51. We have a duty to **care for God's creation**, or as Pope Francis refers to it in *Laudato Si'*, "our common home." We show our respect for the Creator by

our stewardship of God's creation because "every creature is . . . the object of the Father's tenderness, who gives it its place in the world" (*Laudato Si'*, no. 77). **Care for creation** is a duty of our faith and a sign of our concern for all people, especially the poor, who "both everyday experience and scientific research show" suffer "the gravest effects of all attacks on the environment" (no. 48). Pope Francis underscores that environmental degradation can often force the poor "to leave their homes, with great uncertainty for their future and that of their children" (no. 25). The threats to the environment are many. Pope Francis, consistent with both St. John Paul II and Pope Benedict XVI (World Day of Peace Message in 1990 and 2010), has recently lifted up pollution, climate change, lack of access to clean water, and the loss of biodiversity as particular challenges. He speaks of an "ecological debt" (no. 51) owed by wealthier nations to developing nations and he laments the weakness of many responses to the ecological challenges rooted in "complacency and a cheerful recklessness" (no. 59). In the face of this, we should aim for "a new lifestyle" (no. 203-208), one that strives to live simply to meet the needs of the present without compromising the ability of future generations to meet their own needs, and one that brings "healthy pressure to bear on those who wield political, economic and social power." (no. 206). We have a moral obligation to protect the planet on which we live—to respect God's creation and to ensure a safe and hospitable environment for human beings, especially children at their most vulnerable stages of development. As stewards called by God to share the responsibility for the future of the earth, we should work for a world in which people respect and protect all of creation and seek to live simply in harmony with it for the sake of future generations. Fully embracing this task amounts to what Pope Francis calls an "ecological conversion" (no. 219), by which "the effects of [our] encounter with Jesus Christ become evident in [our] relationship with the world around [us]" (no. 217). Such a conversion "can inspire us to greater creativity and enthusiasm in resolving the world's problems and in offering ourselves to God 'as a living sacrifice, holy and acceptable' (Rom 12:1)" (no. 220).

Solidarity

Solidarity highlights in a particular way the intrinsic social nature of the human person, the equality of all in dignity and rights and the common path of individuals and peoples towards an ever more committed unity. . . . Solidarity must be seen above all in its value as a moral virtue that determines the order of institutions. On the

basis of this principle the "structures of sin" (Sollicitudo Rei Socialis, nos. 36, 37)
that dominate relationships between individuals and peoples must be overcome.

(Compendium of the Social Doctrine of the Church, nos. 192-193)

52. We are one human family, whatever our national, racial, ethnic, economic, and ideological differences. We are our brothers' and sisters' keepers, wherever they may be. Loving our neighbor has global dimensions and requires us to eradicate racism and address the extreme poverty and disease plaguing so much of the world. **Solidarity** also includes the scriptural call to welcome the stranger among us—including immigrants seeking work—by ensuring that they have opportunities for a safe home, education for their children, and a decent life for their families and by ending the practice of separating families through deportation. In light of the Gospel's invitation to be peacemakers, our commitment to solidarity with our neighbors—at home and abroad—also demands that we promote peace and pursue justice in a world marred by terrible violence and conflict. Decisions on the use of force should be guided by traditional moral criteria and undertaken only as a last resort. As Bl. Paul VI taught, "If you want peace, work for justice" (*World Day of Peace Message*, January 1, 1972).

53. In reference to solidarity, a special emphasis must be given to the Church's **preferential option for the poor**. While the common good embraces all, those who are weak, vulnerable, and most in need deserve preferential concern. A basic moral test for any society is how it treats those who are most vulnerable. In a society marred by deepening disparities between rich and poor, Sacred Scripture gives us the story of the Last Judgment (see Mt 25:31-46) and reminds us that we will be judged by our response to the "least among us." The *Catechism of the Catholic Church* explains:

> Those who are oppressed by poverty are the object of *a*
> *preferential love* on the part of the Church which, since her
> origin and in spite of the failings of many of her members,
> has not ceased to work for their relief, defense, and liberation
> through numerous works of charity which remain indispens-
> able always and everywhere. (no. 2448)

54. Pope Benedict XVI has taught that "love for widows and orphans, prisoners, and the sick and needy of every kind, is as essential to [the Church] as the

ministry of the sacraments and preaching of the Gospel" (*Deus Caritas Est*, no. 22). This preferential option for the poor and vulnerable includes all who are marginalized in our nation and beyond—unborn children, persons with disabilities, the elderly and terminally ill, victims of injustice and oppression, and immigrants.

55. These four principles and related themes from Catholic social teaching provide a moral framework that does not easily fit ideologies of "right" or "left," "liberal" or "conservative," or the platform of any political party. They are not partisan or sectarian, but reflect fundamental ethical principles that are common to all people.

56. As leaders of the Church in the United States, we bishops have the duty to apply these moral principles to key public policy decisions facing our nation, outlining directions on issues that have important moral and ethical dimensions. More detailed information on policy directions adopted by our bishops' conference can be found in Part II of this document. We hope Catholics and others will seriously consider these policy applications as they make their own decisions in public life.

Conclusion

57. Building a world of respect for human life and dignity, where justice and peace prevail, requires more than just political commitment. Individuals, families, businesses, community organizations, and governments all have a role to play. Participation in political life in light of fundamental moral principles is an essential duty for every Catholic and all people of good will.

58. The Church is involved in the political process but is not partisan. The Church cannot champion any candidate or party. Our cause is the defense of human life and dignity and the protection of the weak and vulnerable.

59. The Church is engaged in the political process but should not be used. We welcome dialogue with political leaders and candidates; we seek to engage and persuade public officials. Events and photo ops cannot substitute for serious dialogue.

60. The Church is principled but not ideological. As St. John Paul II wrote in his encyclical, *Sollicitudo Rei Socialis,*

> The Church's social doctrine is not . . . an ideology, but rather the accurate formulation of the results of a careful reflection on the complex realities of human existence, in society and in the international order, in the light of faith and of the Church's tradition. Its main aim is to interpret these realities, determining their conformity with or divergence from the lines of the Gospel teaching on man and his vocation, a vocation which is at once earthly and transcendent; its aim is thus to guide Christian behavior. It therefore belongs to the field, not of ideology, but of theology and particularly of moral theology. (*Sollicitudo Rei Socialis,* no. 41)

We cannot compromise basic principles or moral teaching. We are committed to clarity about our moral teaching and to civility. In public life, it is important to practice the virtues of charity and justice that are at the core of our Tradition. We should work with others in a variety of ways to advance our moral principles.

61. In light of these principles and the blessings we share as part of a free and democratic nation, we bishops vigorously repeat our call for a renewed kind of politics:

- Focused more on moral principles than on the latest polls

- Focused more on the needs of the weak than on benefits for the strong

- Focused more on the pursuit of the common good than on the demands of narrow interests

62. This kind of political participation reflects the social teaching of our Church and the best traditions of our nation.

PART II

Applying Catholic Teaching to Major Issues: A Summary of Policy Positions of the United States Conference of Catholic Bishops

63. Politics is a noble mission to promote the common good. As such, it is about ethics and principles as well as issues, candidates, and officeholders. To engage in "politics," then, is more than getting involved in current polemics and debates; it is about acting with others and through institutions for the benefit of all. The fact that much of our political rhetoric has become very negative and that political polarization seems to have grown should not dissuade us from the high calling to work for a world that allows everyone to thrive, a world in which all persons, all families, have what they need to fulfill their God-given destiny. In our democracy, one aspect of this task for all of us requires that we weigh issues and related policies. In this brief summary, we bishops call attention to issues with significant moral dimensions that should be carefully considered in each campaign and as policy decisions are made in the years to come. As the descriptions below indicate, some issues involve principles that can never be abandoned, such as the fundamental right to life and marriage as the union of one man and one woman. Others reflect our judgment about the best way to apply Catholic principles to policy issues. No summary could fully reflect the depth and details of the positions taken through the work of the United States Conference of Catholic Bishops (USCCB). While people of good will may sometimes choose different ways to

apply and act on some of our principles, Catholics cannot ignore their inescapable moral challenges or simply dismiss the Church's guidance or policy directions that flow from these principles. For a more complete review of these policy directions and their moral foundations, see the statements listed at the end of this document.

Human Life

64. Our 1998 statement, *Living the Gospel of Life*, declares, "**Abortion and euthanasia** have become preeminent threats to human life and dignity because they directly attack life itself, the most fundamental good and the condition for all others" (no. 5). **Abortion**, the deliberate killing of a human being before birth, is never morally acceptable and must always be opposed. **Cloning** and **destruction of human embryos** for research or even for potential cures are always wrong. The purposeful taking of human life by **assisted suicide and euthanasia** is not an act of mercy, but an unjustifiable assault on human life. **Genocide, torture,** and the **direct and intentional targeting of noncombatants in war or terrorist attacks** are always wrong.

65. Laws that legitimize any of these practices are profoundly unjust and immoral. Our Conference supports laws and policies to protect human life to the maximum degree possible, including constitutional protection for the unborn and legislative efforts to end abortion, assisted suicide, and euthanasia. We also promote a culture of life by supporting laws and programs that encourage childbirth and adoption over abortion and by addressing poverty, providing health care, and offering other assistance to pregnant women, children, and families.

66. The USCCB calls for greater assistance for those who are sick and dying, through health care for all and effective and compassionate palliative care and hospice care. The end of life is a holy moment, a moment that marks a preparation for life with God, and it is to be treated with reverence and accompaniment. The end of life is as sacred as the beginning of life and requires treatment that honors the true dignity of the human person as created in the image of the living God. We recognize that addressing this complex issue effectively will require collaborative efforts between the public and private sectors and across party lines. Policies and decisions regarding **biotechnology** and human experimentation should respect the inherent dignity of human life from its very beginning, regardless of the circumstances of its origin. Respect for human life and dignity is also the foundation for essential efforts to address and overcome the hunger, disease, poverty, and violence that take the lives of so many innocent people.

67. Society has a duty to defend life against violence and to reach out to victims of crime. The Catholic Church has accepted the death penalty in the past for particularly egregious crimes when there was a serious continuing threat to society and no alternative was available. But our nation's continued reliance on the **death penalty** cannot be justified. Because we have other ways to protect society that are more respectful of human life, the USCCB supports efforts to end the use of the death penalty and in the meantime to restrain its use through broader use of DNA evidence, access to effective counsel, and efforts to address unfairness and injustice related to application of the death penalty.

Promoting Peace

68. Catholics must also work **to avoid war and to promote peace**. This is of particular importance, as there is a danger in the present time of becoming indifferent to war because of the number of armed conflicts. War is never a reflection of what ought to be but a sign that something more true to human dignity has failed. The Catholic tradition recognizes the legitimacy of just war teaching when defending the innocent in the face of grave evil, but we must never lose sight of the cost of war and its harm to human life. Nations should protect the dignity of the human person and the right to life by finding more effective ways to prevent conflicts, to resolve them by peaceful means, and to promote reconstruction and reconciliation in the wake of conflicts. Nations have a right and obligation to defend human life and the common good against terrorism, aggression, and similar threats, such as the targeting of persons for persecution because of their religion, including Christians. In the words of Pope Francis, people are being killed "for the sole reason of being Christians" (Homily, Feb. 17, 2015), and there are "more martyrs in the Church today than there were in the first centuries" (Homily, June 30, 2014). "The blood of our Christian brothers and sisters is a testimony which cries out to be heard by everyone who can still distinguish between good and evil. All the more this cry must be heard by those who have the destiny of peoples in their hands" (Message of Pope Francis to Patriarch Abuna Matthias of the Ethiopian Tewahedo Orthodox Church, April 20, 2015). Indeed, the duty of nations to defend human life and the common good demands effective responses to terror, moral assessment of and restraint in the means used, respect for ethical limits on the use of force, a focus on the roots of terror, and fair distribution of the burdens of responding to terror. The use of **torture** must be rejected as fundamentally incompatible with the dignity of the human person and ultimately counterproductive in the effort to combat terrorism. The Church has raised fundamental moral concerns about **preventive use of military force**.[7] Our Church honors the commitment and sacrifice of those who serve in our nation's armed forces

and also recognizes the moral right to conscientious objection to war in general, a particular war, or a military procedure.

69. Even when military force can be justified as a last resort, it should not be indiscriminate or disproportionate. Direct and intentional attacks on noncombatants in war and terrorist acts are never morally acceptable. The use of weapons of mass destruction or other means of warfare that do not distinguish between civilians and soldiers is fundamentally immoral. The United States has a responsibility to work to reverse the spread of **nuclear, chemical, and biological weapons,** and to reduce its own reliance on weapons of mass destruction by pursuing progressive nuclear disarmament. It also must end its use of anti-personnel landmines and reduce its predominant role in the global arms trade. The use of military force confronts us with urgent moral choices. We support the proportionate and discriminate use of military force to protect civilians in a way that recognizes the continuing threat of fanatical extremism and global terror, minimizes the loss of life, and addresses the humanitarian and refugee crises in war-torn regions, and the need to protect human rights, especially religious freedom.

Though we recognize the justifiable use of military force, we encourage the reallocation of resources from armed conflict to the urgent needs of the poor and the root causes of violence. Further, we support policies and actions that protect refugees of war and violence, at home and abroad, and all people suffering religious persecution throughout the world, many of whom are our fellow Christians.

Marriage and Family Life

70. The family founded upon marriage is the basic cell of human society. The role, responsibilities, and needs of families should be central national priorities. **Marriage** must be defined, recognized, and protected as a lifelong exclusive commitment between a man and a woman, and as the source of the next generation and the protective haven for children.[8] The institution of marriage is undermined by the ideology of "gender" that dismisses sexual difference and the complementarity of the sexes and falsely presents "gender" as nothing more than a social construct or psychological reality, which a person may choose at variance with his or her biological reality (see *Compendium of the Social Doctrine of the Church*, no. 224). As Pope Francis has taught, "the removal of [sexual] difference creates a problem, not a solution" (General Audience, April 15, 2015). "Thus the Church reaffirms . . . her no to 'gender' philosophies, because the reciprocity between male and female is an expression of the beauty of nature willed by the Creator" (Pope Benedict XVI,

Address to the Pontifical Council *Cor Unum*, Jan. 19, 2013). This affirmation in no way compromises the Church's opposition to unjust discrimination against those who experience "deep-seated homosexual tendencies," who "must be accepted with respect, compassion, and sensitivity" (*Catechism of the Catholic Church*, no. 2358).

Policies on taxes, work, divorce, immigration, and welfare should uphold the God-given meaning and value of marriage and family, help families stay together, and reward responsibility and sacrifice for children. **Wages** should allow workers to support their families, and public assistance should be available to help poor families to live in dignity. Such assistance should be provided in a manner that promotes eventual financial autonomy.

71. **Children**, in particular, are to be valued, protected, and nurtured. As a Church, we affirm our commitment to the protection and well-being of children in our own institutions and in all of society. Pope Francis has stressed, "Children have a right to grow up in a family with a father and a mother capable of creating a suitable environment for the child's development and emotional maturity" (Address on the Complementarity Between Man and Woman, Nov. 17, 2014). Children who may be placed in foster care or with adoptive parents have a right to be placed in homes with a married man and woman, or if not possible, in environments that do not contradict the authentic meaning of marriage. Child welfare service providers, consistent with their religious beliefs, have a right to place children in such homes rather than in other environments. We oppose contraceptive and abortion mandates in public programs and health plans, which endanger rights of conscience and can interfere with parents' right to guide the moral formation of their children.

Religious Freedom

72. US policy should promote **religious liberty** vigorously, both at home and abroad: our first and most cherished freedom is rooted in the very dignity of the human person, a fundamental human right that knows no geographical boundaries. In all contexts, its basic contours are the same: it is the "immun[ity] from coercion on the part of individuals or of social groups and of any human power, in such wise that no one is to be forced to act in a manner contrary to his own beliefs, whether privately or publicly, whether alone or in association with others, within due limits." (*Dignitatis Humanae*, no. 2). In the United States, religious freedom generally enjoys strong protection in our law and culture, but those protections are now in doubt. For example, the long-standing tax exemption of the Church has been explicitly called into question

at the highest levels of government, precisely because of her teachings on marriage. Catholics have a particular duty to make sure that protections like these do not weaken but instead grow in strength. This is not only to secure the just freedom of the Church and the faithful here but also to offer hope and an encouraging witness to those who suffer direct and even violent religious persecution in countries where the protection is far weaker.

Preferential Option for the Poor and Economic Justice

73. Economic decisions and institutions should be assessed according to whether they protect or undermine the dignity of the human person. Social and economic policies should foster the creation of **jobs for all who can work** with decent working conditions and **just wages**. Barriers to equal pay and employment for women and those facing unjust **discrimination must be overcome**. Catholic social teaching supports the **right of workers to choose whether to organize**, join a union, and bargain collectively, and to exercise these rights without reprisal. It also affirms **economic freedom, initiative, and the right to private property**. Workers, owners, employers, and unions have a corresponding responsibility to work together to create decent jobs, build a more just economy, and advance the common good. We also note with growing concern the increase in "excessive social and economic inequalities," as the *Catechism of the Catholic Church* refers to it, and the shrinking middle class.

74. We support legislation that protects consumers from the excessive and exploitative rates of interest charged by many payday lenders. "Although the quest for equitable profits is acceptable in economic and financial activity, recourse to usury is to be morally condemned" (*Compendium of the Social Doctrine of the Church*, no. 341).

75. **Welfare policy** should reduce **poverty** and dependency, strengthen family life, and help families leave poverty through work, training, and assistance with child care, health care, housing, and transportation. Given the link between family stability and economic success, welfare policy should address both the economic and cultural factors that contribute to family breakdown. It should also provide a safety net for those who cannot work. Improving the **Earned Income Tax Credit** and **child tax credits**, available as refunds to families in greatest need, will help lift low-income families out of poverty.

76. **Faith-based groups** deserve recognition and support, not as a substitute for government, but as responsive, effective partners, especially in the poorest communities and countries. The USCCB actively supports conscience clauses

and other religious freedom protections, opposes any effort to undermine the ability of faith-based groups to preserve their identity and integrity as partners with government, and is committed to protecting long-standing civil rights and other protections for both religious groups and the people they serve. Government bodies should not require Catholic institutions to compromise their moral or religious convictions to participate in government health or human service programs.

77. **Social Security** should provide adequate, continuing, and reliable income in an equitable manner for low- and average-wage workers and their families when these workers retire or become disabled, and for the survivors when a wage-earner dies.

78. The lack of safe, affordable **housing** requires a renewed commitment to increase the supply of quality housing and to preserve, maintain, and improve existing housing through public/private partnerships, especially with religious groups and community organizations. The USCCB continues to oppose unjust housing discrimination and to support measures to meet the credit needs of low-income and minority communities.

79. A first priority for **agriculture** policy should be **food security for all**. Because no one should face **hunger** in a land of plenty, the Supplemental Nutrition Assistance Program (SNAP or Food Stamps), the Special Nutrition Program for Women, Infants, and Children (WIC), and other nutrition programs need to be strong and effective. Farmers and farm workers who grow, harvest, and process food deserve a just return for their labor, with safe and just working conditions and adequate housing. Supporting rural communities sustains a way of life that enriches our nation. Careful stewardship of the earth and its natural resources demands policies that support **sustainable agriculture** as vital elements of agricultural policy.

Health Care

80. **Affordable and accessible health care** is an essential safeguard of human life and a fundamental human right. Despite an increase in the number of people insured, millions of Americans still lack health care coverage. Health care coverage remains an urgent national priority. The nation's health care system needs to be rooted in values that respect human dignity, protect human life, respect the principle of subsidiarity, and meet the needs of the poor and uninsured, especially born and unborn children, pregnant women, immigrants, and other vulnerable populations. Employers, including religious groups

and family-owned businesses, should be able to provide health care without compromising their moral or religious convictions, and individuals should be able to purchase health care that accords with their faith. The USCCB supports measures to strengthen Medicare and Medicaid. Our conference also advocates effective, compassionate care that reflects Catholic moral values for those suffering from HIV/AIDS and those coping with addictions.

Migration

81. The Gospel mandate to "welcome the stranger" requires Catholics to care for and stand with **newcomers**, authorized and unauthorized, including unaccompanied immigrant children, refugees and asylum-seekers, those unnecessarily detained, and victims of human trafficking. Comprehensive reform is urgently necessary to fix a broken immigration system and should include a broad and fair legalization program with a path to citizenship; a work program with worker protections and just wages; family reunification policies; access to legal protections, which include due process procedures; refuge for those fleeing persecution and violence; and policies to address the root causes of migration. The right and responsibility of nations to control their borders and to maintain the rule of law should be recognized but pursued in a just and humane manner. The detention of immigrants should be used to protect public safety and not for purposes of deterrence or punishment; alternatives to detention, including community-based programs, should be emphasized.

　　As Pope Francis has said, human trafficking is a "crime against humanity" (Address, Dec. 12, 2013, and April 10, 2014) and should be eradicated from the earth. Trafficking victims, most especially children, should receive care and protection, including special consideration for permanent legal status. Additional education and mobilization efforts are needed to address the root causes of human trafficking—poverty, conflict, and the breakdown of judicial process in source countries.

Catholic Education

82. Parents—the first and most important educators—have a fundamental **right to choose the education** best suited to the needs of their children, including public, private, and religious schools. Government, through such means as tax credits and publicly funded scholarships, should help provide resources for parents, especially those of modest means, to exercise this basic right without discrimination. Students in all educational settings should have

opportunities for moral and character formation consistent with the beliefs and responsibilities of their parents.

83. All persons have a right to receive a quality **education**. Young people, including those who are poor and those with disabilities, need to have the opportunity to develop intellectually, morally, spiritually, and physically, allowing them to become good citizens who make socially and morally responsible decisions. This requires parental choice in education. It also requires educational institutions to have orderly, just, respectful, and non-violent environments where adequate professional and material resources are available. The USCCB strongly supports adequate funding, including scholarships, tax credits, and other means, to educate all persons no matter what their personal condition or what school they attend—public, private, or religious. All teachers and administrators deserve salaries and benefits that reflect principles of economic justice, as well as access to resources necessary for teachers to prepare for their important tasks. Services aimed at improving education—especially for those most at risk—that are available to students and teachers in public schools should also be available to students and teachers in **private and religious schools** as a matter of justice.

Promoting Justice and Countering Violence

84. Promoting moral responsibility and effective responses to violent crime, curbing violence in media, supporting reasonable restrictions on access to assault weapons and handguns, and opposing the use of the **death penalty** are particularly important in light of a growing "culture of violence." An ethic of responsibility, rehabilitation, and restoration should be a foundation for the reform of our broken **criminal justice system**. A humane and remedial rather than a strictly punitive approach to offenders should be developed. Such an approach includes supporting efforts that justly reduce the prison population, help people leaving prison to reintegrate into their communities, combat recidivism, promote just sentencing reform, and strengthen relationships between the police and the communities they serve.

Combatting Unjust Discrimination

85. It is important for our society to continue to combat any unjust **discrimination, whether** based on race, religion, sex, ethnicity, disabling condition, or age, as these are grave injustices and affronts to human dignity. Where the effects of past discrimination persist, society has the obligation to take positive

steps to overcome the legacy of injustice, including vigorous action to remove barriers to education, protect voting rights, support good policing in our communities, and ensure equal employment for women and minorities.

Care for Our Common Home

86. **Care for Creation** is a moral issue. Protecting the land, water, and air we share is a religious duty of stewardship and reflects our responsibility to born and unborn children, who are most vulnerable to environmental assault. We must answer the question that Pope Francis posed to the world: "What kind of world do we want to leave to those who come after us, to children who are now growing up?" (*Laudato Si'*, no. 160). There are many concrete steps we can take to assure justice and solidarity between the generations. Effective initiatives are required for energy conservation and the development of alternate, renewable, and clean-energy resources. Our Conference offers a distinctive call to seriously address **global climate change**, focusing on the virtue of prudence, pursuit of the common good, and the impact on the poor, particularly on vulnerable workers and the poorest nations. The United States should lead in contributing to the sustainable development of poorer nations and promoting greater justice in sharing the burden of environmental blight, neglect, and recovery. It is important that we address the rising number of migrants who are uprooted from their homeland as a consequence of environmental degradation and climate change. They are not currently recognized as refugees under any existing international convention and are thus not afforded legal protections that ought to be due to them.

Our nation's efforts to reduce poverty should not be associated with demeaning and sometimes coercive population control programs. Such an approach is condemned by Pope Francis:

> Instead of resolving the problems of the poor and thinking of how the world can be different, some can only propose a reduction in the birth rate. At times, developing countries face forms of international pressure which make economic assistance contingent on certain policies of "reproductive health." Yet "while it is true that an unequal distribution of the population and of available resources creates obstacles to development and a sustainable use of the environment,

it must nonetheless be recognized that demographic growth is fully compatible with an integral and shared development" (*Compendium of the Social Doctrine of the Church*, no. 483). To blame population growth, instead of an extreme and selective consumerism on the part of some, is one way of refusing to face the issues. It is an attempt to legitimize the present model of distribution, where a minority believes that it has the right to consume in a way which can never be universalized, since the planet could not even contain the waste products of such consumption. Besides, we know that approximately a third of all food produced is discarded, and "whenever food is thrown out it is as if were stolen from the table of the poor" (Catechesis, June 5, 2013). (*Laudato Si'*, no. 50)

Our efforts should, instead, focus on working with the poor to help them build a future of hope and opportunity for themselves and their children.

Communications, Media, and Culture

87. Print, broadcast, and electronic **media** shape the culture. To protect children and families, responsible regulation is needed that respects freedom of speech yet also addresses policies that have lowered standards, permitted increasingly offensive material, and reduced opportunities for non-commercial religious programming.

88. Regulation should limit concentration of media control, resist management that is primarily focused on profit, and encourage a variety of program sources, including religious programming. TV rating systems and appropriate technology can assist parents in supervising what their children view.

89. The Internet offers both great benefits and significant problems. The benefits should be available to all students regardless of income. Because access to pornographic and violent material is becoming easier, vigorous enforcement of obscenity and child pornography laws is necessary, as well as technology that assists parents, schools, and libraries in blocking unwanted or undesirable materials.

Global Solidarity

90. The increasing interconnectedness of our world calls for a moral response, the virtue of solidarity. In the words of St. John Paul II, "Solidarity is a firm and persevering determination to commit oneself to the common good" (*Sollicitudo Rei Socialis*, no. 38). A more just world will likely be a more peaceful world, a world less vulnerable to terrorism and other violence. The United States has the responsibility to take the lead in addressing the scandal of **poverty and underdevelopment.** Our nation should help to **humanize globalization**, addressing its negative consequences and spreading its benefits, especially among the world's poor. The United States also has a unique opportunity to use its power in partnership with others to build a more just and peaceful world.

- The United States should take a leading role in helping to **alleviate global poverty** through substantially increased development aid for the poorest countries, more equitable trade policies, and continuing efforts to relieve the crushing burdens of debt and disease.

- US policy should promote **religious liberty** and other basic **human rights**. In particular, US policy should promote and defend the rights of religious minorities throughout the world, especially in regions where people of faith are threatened by violence simply because of their faith.

- The United States should provide political and financial support for beneficial **United Nations** programs and reforms, for other **international bodies**, and for international law, so that together these institutions may become more responsible and responsive agents for addressing global problems.

- Asylum should be afforded to refugees who hold a well-founded fear of persecution in their homelands. Our country should support protection for persons fleeing persecution through safe haven in other countries, including the United States, especially for unaccompanied children, women, victims of human trafficking, and religious minorities.

faithful citizenship

- Our country should be a leader—in collaboration with the international community—in addressing **regional conflicts**.

- Leadership on the **Israeli-Palestinian conflict** is an especially urgent priority. The United States should actively pursue comprehensive negotiations leading to a just and peaceful resolution that respects the legitimate claims and aspirations of both Israelis and Palestinians, ensuring security for Israel, a viable state for Palestinians, respect for Lebanon's sovereignty, and peace in the region. Defending human life, building peace, combating poverty and despair, and protecting freedom and human rights are not only moral imperatives—they are wise national priorities that will make our nation and world safer.

PART III

★ ★ ★

Goals for Political Life: Challenges for Citizens, Candidates, and Public Officials

91. As Catholics, we are led to raise questions for political life other than those that concentrate on individual, material well-being. Our focus is not on party affiliation, ideology, economics, or even competence and capacity to perform duties, as important as such issues are. Rather, we focus on what protects or threatens the dignity of every human life.

92. Catholic teaching challenges voters and candidates, citizens and elected officials, to consider the moral and ethical dimensions of public policy issues. In light of ethical principles, we bishops offer the following policy goals that we hope will guide Catholics as they form their consciences and reflect on the moral dimensions of their public choices. Not all issues are equal; these ten goals address matters of different moral weight and urgency. Some involve intrinsically evil acts, which can never be approved. Others involve affirmative obligations to seek the common good. These and similar goals can help voters and candidates act on ethical principles rather than particular interests and partisan allegiances. We hope Catholics will ask candidates how they intend to help our nation pursue these important goals:

> Address the preeminent requirement to protect the weakest in our midst—innocent unborn children—by restricting and bringing to an end the destruction of unborn children through abortion and providing women in crisis pregnancies the supports they need to make a decision for life.

- Keep our nation from turning to violence to address fundamental problems—a million abortions each year to deal with unwanted pregnancies, euthanasia and assisted suicide to deal with the burdens of illness and disability, the destruction of human embryos in the name of research, the use of the death penalty to combat crime, and imprudent resort to war to address international disputes.

- Protect the fundamental understanding of marriage as the life-long and faithful union of one man and one woman and as the central institution of society; promote the complementarity of the sexes and reject false "gender" ideologies; and provide better support for family life morally, socially, and economically, so that our nation helps parents raise their children with respect for life, sound moral values, and an ethic of stewardship and responsibility.

- Achieve comprehensive immigration reform that offers a path to citizenship, treats immigrant workers fairly, prevents the separation of families, maintains the integrity of our borders, respects the rule of law, and addresses the factors that compel people to leave their own countries.

- Help families and children overcome poverty: ensuring access to and choice in education, as well as decent work at fair, living wages and adequate assistance for the vulnerable in our nation, while also helping to overcome widespread hunger and poverty around the world, especially in the areas of development assistance, debt relief, and international trade.

- Provide health care while respecting human life, human dignity, and religious freedom in our health care system.

- Continue to oppose policies that reflect prejudice, hostility toward immigrants, religious bigotry, and other forms of unjust discrimination.

- Encourage families, community groups, economic structures, and government to work together to overcome poverty, pursue the common good, and care for creation, with full respect for individuals and groups and their right to address social needs in accord with their basic moral and religious convictions.

faithful citizenship

- Establish and comply with moral limits on the use of military force—examining for what purposes it may be used, under what authority, and at what human cost—with a special view to seeking a responsible and effective response for ending the persecution of Christians and other religious minorities in the Middle East and other parts of the world.

- Join with others around the world to pursue peace, protect human rights and religious liberty, and advance economic justice and care for creation.

Notes

1   The common good is "the sum total of social conditions which allow people, either as groups or as individuals, to reach their fulfillment more fully and more easily" (*Catechism of the Catholic Church*, no. 1906).

2   "Ignorance of Christ and his Gospel, bad example given by others, enslavement to one's passions, assertion of a mistaken notion of autonomy of conscience, rejection of the Church's authority and her teaching, lack of conversion and charity: these can be at the source of errors of judgment in moral conduct" (*Catechism of the Catholic Church*, no. 1792).

3   "When political activity comes up against moral principles that do not admit of exception, compromise, or derogation, the Catholic commitment becomes more evident and laden with responsibility. In the face of *fundamental and inalienable ethical demands*, Christians must recognize that what is at stake is the essence of the moral law, which concerns the integral good of the human person. This is the case with laws concerning *abortion* and *euthanasia*. . . . Such laws must defend the basic right to life from conception to natural death" (*Doctrinal Note on Some Questions Regarding the Participation of Catholics in Political Life*, no. 4).

4   See *Catechism of the Catholic Church*, no. 2297.

5   These themes are drawn from a rich tradition of principles and ideas that are more fully described in the *Compendium of the Social Doctrine of the Church* from the Pontifical Council for Justice and Peace (Washington, DC: United States Conference of Catholic Bishops, 2005).

6   See *Catechism of the Catholic Church*, no. 2297.

7   See *Compendium of the Social Doctrine of the Church*, no. 501.

8   See *Considerations Regarding Proposals to Give Legal Recognition to Unions Between Homosexual Persons*.

References

Catechism of the Catholic Church (2nd ed.). Washington, DC: Libreria Editrice Vaticana–United States Conference of Catholic Bishops (USCCB), 2000.

Pope Francis. *Laudato Si' (On Care for Our Common Home)*. Washington, DC: USCCB, 2015.

Pope Francis. *Evangelii Gaudium (The Joy of the Gospel)*. Washington, DC: USCCB, 2013.

Pope Benedict XVI. *Caritas in Veritate (Charity in Truth)*. Washington, DC: USCCB, 2009.

Congregation for the Doctrine of the Faith. *Doctrinal Note on Some Questions Regarding the Participation of Catholics in Political Life*. In *Readings on Catholics in Political Life*. Washington, DC: USCCB, 2006.

Congregation for the Doctrine of the Faith. *Considerations Regarding Proposals to Give Legal Recognition to Unions Between Homosexual Persons*, 2003.

Pope Benedict XVI. *Deus Caritas Est (God Is Love)*. Washington, DC: USCCB, 2006.

Pope Benedict XVI. *Sacramentum Caritatis (The Sacrament of Charity)*. Washington, DC: USCCB, 2007.

Pope John XXIII. *Pacem in Terris (Peace on Earth)*. Washington, DC: USCCB, 1963.

Pope John Paul II. *Christifideles Laici (On the Vocation and the Mission of the Lay Faithful in the Church and in the World)*. Washington, DC: USCCB, 1989.

Pope John Paul II. *Evangelium Vitae (The Gospel of Life)*. Washington, DC: USCCB, 1995.

Pope John Paul II. *Veritatis Splendor* (*The Splendor of Truth*). Washington, DC: USCCB, 1993.

Second Vatican Council. *Dignitatis Humanae* (*Declaration on Religious Liberty*). Vatican website.

Second Vatican Council. *Gaudium et Spes* (*Pastoral Constitution on the Church in the Modern World*). Vatican website.

USCCB. *Living the Gospel of Life: A Challenge to American Catholics*. Washington, DC: USCCB, 1998.

Major Catholic Statements on Public Life and Moral Issues

The following documents from the United States Conference of Catholic Bishops (USCCB) explore in greater detail the public policy issues discussed in *Forming Consciences for Faithful Citizenship*. The documents are listed chronologically, except for under the first heading, where they are grouped generally by topic and then by year.

For more information on these and other documents, visit the USCCB website: *www.usccb.org*. Documents marked with an asterisk are not available online.

Protecting Human Life

Life-Giving Love in an Age of Technology, 2009

Married Love and the Gift of Life, 2006

On Embryonic Stem Cell Research, 2008

Pastoral Plan for Pro-Life Activities: A Campaign in Support of Life, 2001

Living the Gospel of Life: A Challenge to American Catholics, 1998

Faithful for Life: A Moral Reflection, 1995

A Matter of the Heart: A Statement on the Thirtieth Anniversary of Roe v. Wade, 2002

Resolution on Abortion, 1989

Documentation on the Right to Life and Abortion, 1974, 1976, 1981*

A Call for Bipartisan Cooperation on Responsible Transition in Iraq, 2007

Statement on Iraq, 2002

A Pastoral Message: Living with Faith and Hope After September 11, 2001

Sowing the Weapons of War, 1995

The Harvest of Justice Is Sown in Peace, 1993

A Report on the Challenge of Peace and Policy Developments, 1983-1888, 1989*

The Challenge of Peace: God's Promise and Our Response, 1983

To Live Each Day with Dignity: A Statement on Physician-Assisted Suicide, 2011

Nutrition and Hydration: Moral and Pastoral Reflections, 1992*

Statement on Euthanasia, 1991

Welcome and Justice for Persons with Disabilities, 1999*

Pastoral Statement of United States Catholic Bishops on Persons with Disabilities, 1984*

Confronting a Culture of Violence, 1995

A Culture of Life and the Penalty of Death, 2005

Statement on Capital Punishment, 1980

Ethical and Religious Directives for Catholic Health Care Services (Fifth Edition), 2009

Promoting Family Life

Marriage: Love and Life in the Divine Plan, 2009

National Directory for Catechesis, 2005*

Renewing Our Commitment to Catholic Elementary and Secondary Schools in the Third Millennium, 2005

Sharing Catholic Social Teaching: Challenges and Directions, 1998

Principles for Educational Reform in the United States, 1995*

To Teach as Jesus Did: A Pastoral Message on Catholic Education, 1972*

When I Call for Help: A Pastoral Response to Domestic Violence Against Women, 2002

A Family Perspective in Church and Society, 1998

Blessings of Age, 1999

Between Man and Woman: Questions and Answers About Marriage and Same-Sex Unions, 2003

Walk in the Light: A Pastoral Response to Child Sexual Abuse, 1995

Follow the Way of Love: A Pastoral Message to Families, 1993

Putting Children and Families First: A Challenge for Our Church, Nation and World, 1992*

Pursuing Social Justice

Ethical and Religious Directives for Catholic Health Care Services (Fifth Edition), 2009

For I Was Hungry and You Gave Me Food: Catholic Reflections on Food, Farmers and Farmworkers, 2003

Strangers No Longer: Together on the Journey of Hope, 2003

A Place at the Table: A Catholic Recommitment to Overcome Poverty and to Respect the Dignity of All God's Children, 2002

Global Climate Change: A Plea for Dialogue, Prudence, and the Common Good, 2001

Responsibility, Rehabilitation, and Restoration: A Catholic Perspective on Crime and Criminal Justice, 2000

A Commitment to All Generations: Social Security and the Common Good, 1999

In All Things Charity: A Pastoral Challenge for the New Millennium, 1999

One Family Under God, 1995*

Confronting a Culture of Violence: A Catholic Framework for Action, 1995

Moral Principles and Policy Priorities for Welfare Reform, 1995*

The Harvest of Justice Is Sown in Peace, 1993

A Framework for Comprehensive Health Care Reform, 1993*

Renewing the Earth: An Invitation to Reflection and Action on the Environment in Light of Catholic Social Teaching, 1992

Putting Children and Families First: A Challenge for Our Church, Nation and World, 1992*

New Slavery, New Freedom: A Pastoral Message on Substance Abuse, 1990*

Brothers and Sisters to Us: Pastoral Letter on Racism in Our Day, 1989

Called to Compassion and Responsibility: A Response to the HIV/AIDS Crisis, 1989

Homelessness and Housing: A Human Tragedy, A Moral Challenge, 1988*

Practicing Global Solidarity

A Call for Bipartisan Cooperation on Responsible Transition in Iraq, 2007

A Call to Solidarity with Africa, 2001

A Jubilee Call for Debt Forgiveness, 1999

Called to Global Solidarity: International Challenges for US Parishes, 1998

Sowing the Weapons of War, 1995

One Family Under God, 1995*

The Harvest of Justice Is Sown in Peace, 1993

The New Moment in Eastern and Central Europe, 1990*

Toward Peace in the Middle East, 1989

Statement on Central America, 1987

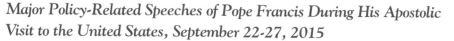

Major Policy-Related Speeches of Pope Francis During His Apostolic Visit to the United States, September 22-27, 2015

Pope Francis. Address of the Holy Father, Welcoming Ceremony, South Lawn of the White House, Washington, DC, September 23, 2015. *http:// w2.vatican.va/content/francesco/en/speeches/2015/september/documents/papa-francesco_20150923_usa-benvenuto.html*

Pope Francis, Address of the Holy Father, Visit to the Joint Session of the United States Congress, United States Capitol, Washington, DC, September 24, 2015. *http://w2.vatican.va/content/francesco/en/speeches/2015/september/documents/papa-francesco_20150924_usa-us-congress.html*

Pope Francis. Address of the Holy Father, Meeting with the Members of the General Assembly of the United Nations Organization, United Nations Headquarters, New York City. September 25, 2015. *http://w2.vatican.va/content/francesco/en/speeches/2015/september/documents/papa-francesco_20150925_onu-visita.html*

Pope Francis. Address of the Holy Father, Meeting for Religious Liberty with the Hispanic Community and Other Immigrants, Independence Mall, Philadelphia. September 26, 2015. *http://w2.vatican.va/content/francesco/en/speeches/2015/september/documents/papa-francesco_20150926_usa-liberta-religiosa.html*